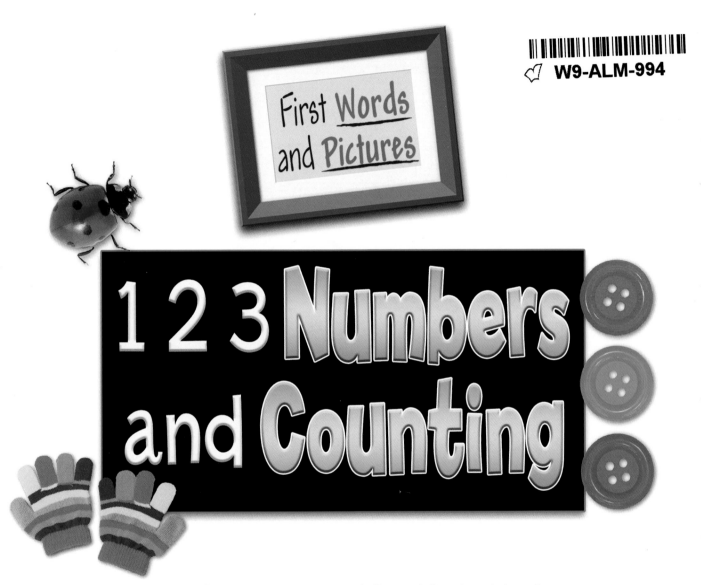

First Words and Pictures

1 2 3 Numbers and Counting

By Ruth Owen, Emma Randall, and Sophie Murphy

Ruby Tuesday Books

Published in 2017 by Ruby Tuesday Books Ltd.

Copyright © 2017 Ruby Tuesday Books Ltd.

Editor: Mark J. Sachner
Production: John Lingham

Photo Credits:
Photographs courtesy of Shutterstock

Library of Congress Control Number: 2017908516

Print ISBN: 978-1-911341-79-6
eBook ISBN: 978-1-911341-80-2

Printed and published in the United States of America

For further information including rights and permissions requests, please contact our Customer Service Department at 877-377-8577.

What's Inside the Book?

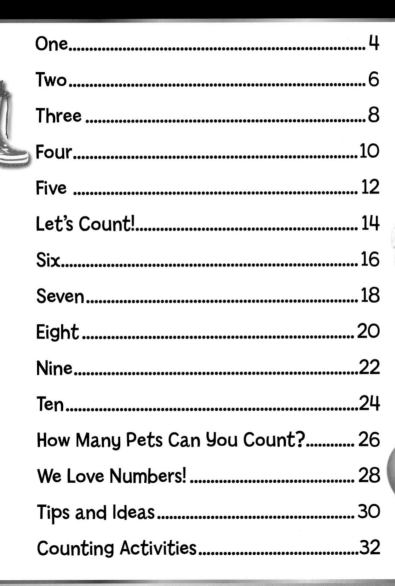

cow

calf

1 one

lamb

sheep

4

horse

foal

chicken

piglet

pig

chick

egg

dress

2 two

glove

sock

6

T-shirt

hat

a pair of shoes

Two things that look the
same make a pair.
Can you point to some
other pairs?

boot

jeans

soccer ball

tennis ball

basketball

3 three

crayons

fairies

dinosaurs

teddy bears

Count out loud the number of teddy bears.

bricks

dolls

9

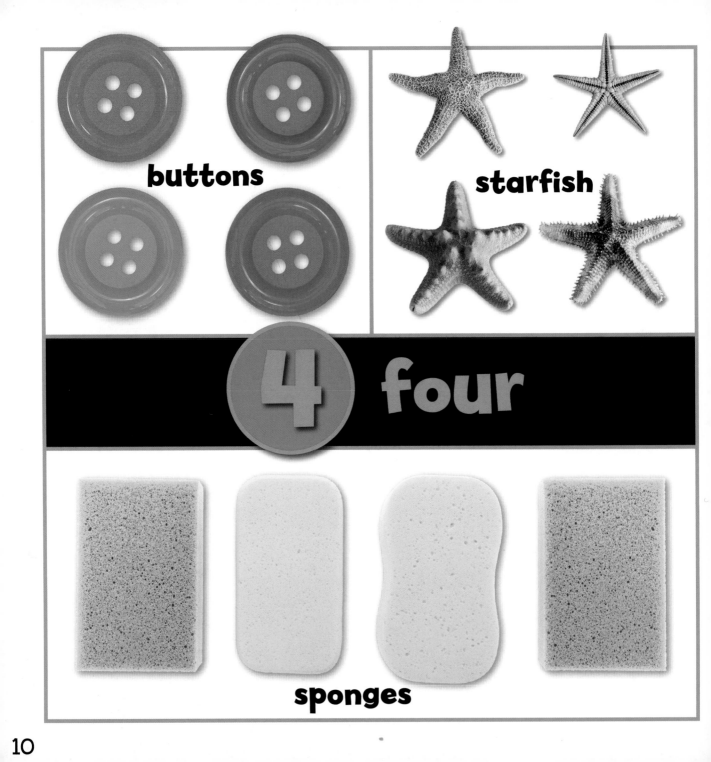

buttons

starfish

4 four

sponges

10

hearts

sandwiches

blocks

If you eat
one sandwich,
how many will be left?

five

Happy birthday!

balloons

presents

cupcakes

lollipops

candle

How many candles are on the birthday cake?

fingers

hand

Let's Count!

1 2 3 4 5

1 cookie

2 halves

3 owls

elephant

How many legs does the elephant have?

2 ears

2 eyes

1 mouth

1 nose

1 2 3 4 5

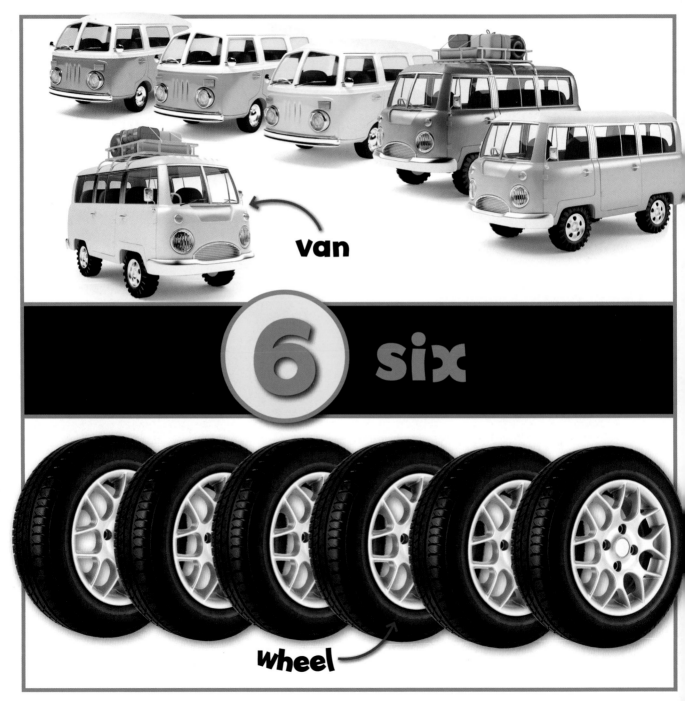

van

6 six

wheel

How many cars can you count?

car

How many red cars are there?

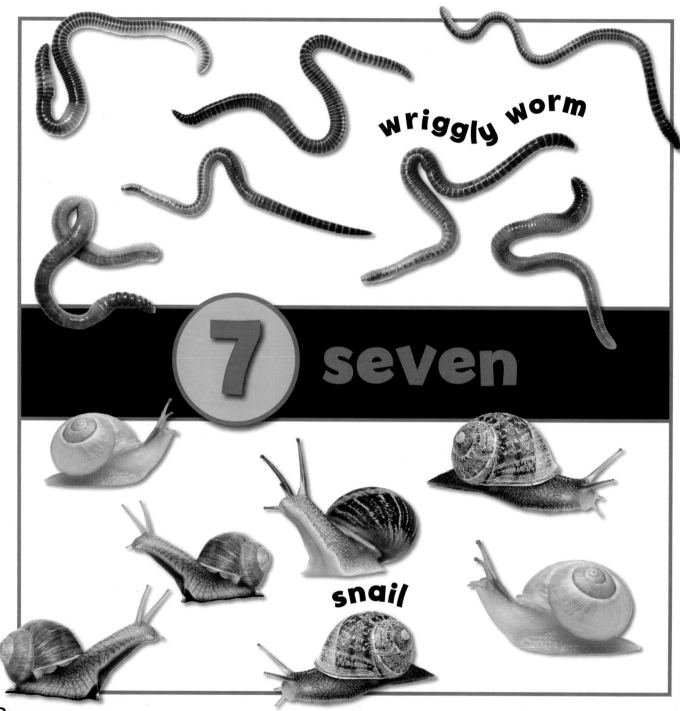

wriggly worm

7 seven

snail

ladybug

How many shiny beetles do you see?

beetle

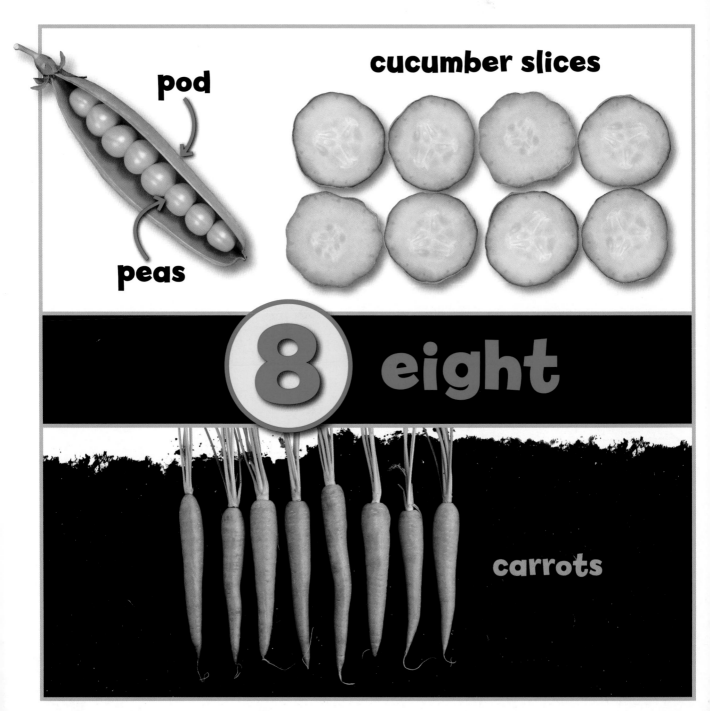

pod

peas

cucumber slices

8 eight

carrots

broccoli

tangerine

peeled

strawberries

If you give half of the strawberries to a friend, how many will you each have?

9 nine

leaf

How many flowers can you count?

flower

How many yellow flowers are there?

23

10 ten

Count out loud the number of happy monsters.

monster

1   2   3   4   5

24

ice cream truck

forklift

tractor

dump truck

10 busy vehicles

bus

delivery van

fire engine

semi-truck

digger

cement mixer

6   7   8   9   10

dog

puppy

How Many Pets Can You Count?

cat

kitten

1 2 3 4 5 6 7 8 9 10

26

fish

hamster

guinea pig

rabbit

11 12 13 14 15 16 17 18 19 20

27

a pair of feet

toe

How many toes can you count?

We Love Numbers!

2 kittens + 1 kitten

How many kittens?

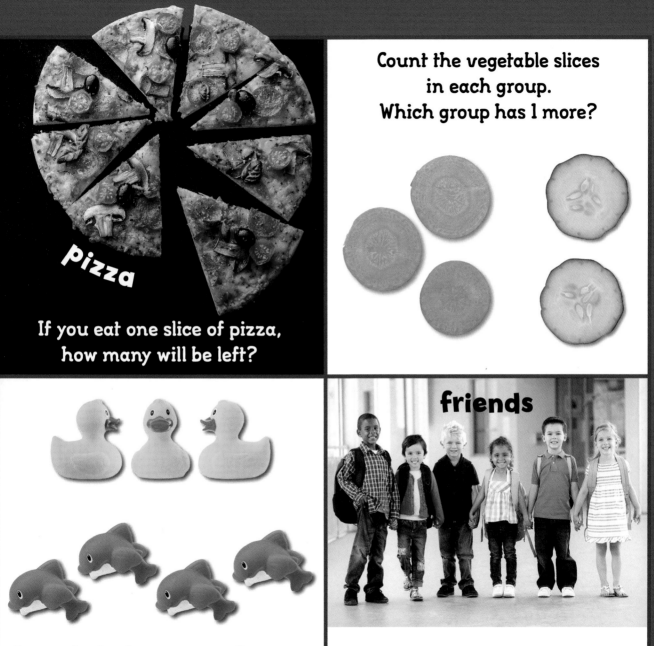

pizza

If you eat one slice of pizza,
how many will be left?

Count the vegetable slices
in each group.
Which group has 1 more?

Count the bath toys in each group.
Which group has 1 less?

friends

How many friends do you see?

Tips and Ideas

Look ✓ Read ✓ Talk ✓ Discover ✓ Learn ✓

This book is designed to help you and your child get the best learning experience possible. We suggest that you make yourselves comfortable within a quiet environment and allow your child to hold the book and turn the pages. When you and your child are reading the book, pause to allow your child to *read* a word or ask questions about the pictures and words.

Pages 4-5: Ask your child to point to the pictures and together read the animal words and the number 1 out loud. For example: one pig, one cow, one foal, etc. Hold up one finger to show your child the number 1.

Pages 6-7: The concept of pairs can be difficult for young children to understand. Begin your child's understanding of pairs by using the pictures on these pages. When TWO things look the same and are used together (for example, socks, shoes, and gloves), they make a PAIR. We also use the word "pair" to describe the jeans because a pair of jeans has TWO legs.

Pages 8-9: If your child is just starting to count, collect three of your child's toys (balls, teddy bears, or dolls). Count upward as you put the toys in a line in front of your child. Show your child the corresponding picture in the book and count the three toys out loud. Say: *We have 1, 2, 3 balls. Look, there are 1, 2, 3 balls in the picture.*

Pages 10-11: To help your child with subtraction, first ask him or her to count the four sandwiches. Next, say: *If you subtract (or take away) one sandwich, you will have 1, 2, 3 sandwiches* (cover one sandwich with your hand and point to the other sandwiches in turn to aid your child's thinking).

The pictures on these pages can also be used for teaching about shapes (circles, stars, rectangles, hearts, triangles, and squares).

Pages 12-13: Ask your child how old he or she is. Get your child to show you their age by using their fingers. How old will your child be on their next birthday?

Pages 14-15: Use your fingers to help your child practice counting. For example, raise one finger and say to your child: *I have ONE finger up.* Next put up THREE more fingers, explaining what you are doing. Ask your child to point at your fingers and count out loud how many fingers you are now holding up.

Point to the girl's face and explain that a person has a PAIR of eyes. What else comes in pairs on our heads? (Ears, eyebrows, and cheeks.) This can be extended to other body parts, such as hands, arms, legs, and feet.

Pages 16-17: Use the car pictures to help your child practice his or her adding skills. For example: If there are 3 red cars and 1 green car, how many cars are there?

Pages 18-19: Practice adding with wriggly worms. Ask your child to draw 2 worms. Then ask him or her to draw 2 more worms. Say to your child: *How many worms have you drawn?*

Pages 20-21: Use the tangerine picture, or a real tangerine, to explain sharing. Say: *We have ONE tangerine and we peel off its skin. There are EIGHT pieces. Share the pieces between FOUR people. How many would each person have?*

To help with subtracting say: *If you eat TWO strawberries, how many will be left?*

Page 23: Explain to your child that the flowers have different numbers of petals. Ask your child to draw a flower with petals. Then ask your child to count how many petals he or she has drawn. If your child has drawn more petals than he or she can count, help with the counting process.

Page 24: Explain to your child that some of the monsters have more or less than one PAIR of eyes. Ask your child to point to the monsters that have: one eye, a PAIR of eyes, and two PAIRS of eyes.

Counting Activities

Let's Practice Counting

Take six buttons (or small objects for counting) and a muffin pan (or any object with clear divisions). Place one button into each of six pan sections. Ask your child to count how many buttons are in the pan. Remove TWO buttons and ask your child to count again. Explain that you had SIX buttons but you now have FOUR because you took away TWO. Add ONE more button, while explaining what you are doing. Then ask your child to count how many buttons you have now. Continue this adding and subtracting game, removing and adding buttons to the pan.

Recognizing Numbers

Collect 15 toy blocks. Write the numbers 1 to 5 on five sheets of paper, using one sheet for each number. Ask your child to look at each number and then place that number of blocks on the sheet of paper. If your child struggles with this, count the number of blocks out loud with him or her while placing them on the paper.

Toys and Numbers I SPY

Collect 15 toys in five groups. For example: 5 cars, 4 teddy bears, 3 dolls, 2 balls, and 1 toy farm animal. Draw a checklist that shows the toys and the number. Place all the toys in a box.

Ask your child what he or she sees on the checklist. Once your child has named a toy, encourage him or her to notice the number next to the toy. Then say: *Yes, there is a picture of a car. The number 5 is next to the car. Can you find 5 cars in the box?*

Once your child has found and counted 5 cars, check off this item on the list. Continue to encourage number recognition throughout the game.